Slender Certainties

Other Books of Poetry
by Mary Lou Soutar-Hynes

Any Waking Morning (2019, Inanna)

Dark Water Songs (2013, Inanna)

Travelling Light (2006, Seraphim Editions)

The Fires of Naming (2001, Seraphim Editions)

Slender Certainties

Mary Lou Soutar-Hynes

Aeolus House

Cover Design and Typography: McNeill Design Arts
Cover Photo: J. Davidson-Palmer, "Stairway to the Unknown,"
Copyright ©2025 J. Davidson-Palmer, www.judithdavidsonpalmer.com
Author Photo: J. Davidson-Palmer
Editor: Allan Briesmaster

Library and Archives Canada Cataloguing in Publication

Title: Slender certainties / Mary Lou Soutar-Hynes.
Names: Soutar-Hynes, Mary Lou, author
Identifiers: Canadiana (print) 20260238317 | Canadiana (ebook) 0260238325 | ISBN 9781834210360 | ISBN 9781834210377 (EPUB) | ISBN 9781834210599 (PDF) ver)
:3
Subjects: LCGFT: Poetry.
Classification: LCC PS8587.O9756 S54 2026 | DDC C811/.6—dc23

A co-publication between Inanna Publications and Aeolus House

Published by
Aeolus House
P.O. Box 53031
Royal Orchard Postal Station
10 Royal Orchard Blvd.
Thornhill, ON L3T 3C0
www.aeolushouse.com

Printed in Canada

for Anne-Marie

Contents

Preface

Each new poetry collection reveals its own unique shape as poems, sometimes spanning years, are harvested, rub shoulders, move around, and settle in side-by-side. I feel particularly blessed to be able to share this one. In the summer of 2019, I suffered a stroke. It had a definite poetry connection, occurring as it did on the last day of the League of Canadian Poets' annual conference in St. John's, Nfld. I was in my hotel room, preparing to introduce my recently published fourth collection, *Any Waking Morning*, at the members' reading later that day.

The stroke was a paradigm-shifting experience, where time tilted and certainties dissolved. Since then, I've seen each day through mortality's sharpened lens. This perspective has focused the collection and has influenced its field of view. While poems more specifically referencing the stroke experience appear nearer the end, the entire collection bears its fingerprints, and is refracted through its lens.

Mary Lou Soutar-Hynes
March, 2025

In the art

of measuring
it seems we're all horologists —
time's
tick tock tick
marked, sprung, hands
& dials —
hearts like clocks

all rhythms & eddies
self-sustained & pulsatile, assuming
no resistance — incompressible
always at-the-ready — poised
for heart-beat's
thrum

I: Subtle Alchemies

She is susceptible

to sunlight
its singular vocabulary —

arc of winter's warm reprieve
peppermint & sage

dark matter's casual intensity
harmonics of a wave

twilight minutes beyond the cedars
ebb and flow of a gaze

those shimmering spaces
their questions locked   like rooms

Sight-lines

I took one look and fell, hook
and tumble
— Mary Oliver

along a mirror's plane
door ajar —
your breath,   or was it hers,   the quality
of light —
and falling
hook & tumble

angles of incidence
tight-turns   and paths revealed
in the fullness
of years —   reflection's
piercing certainty —   and you,   enthralled
counting the ways

of milkweed
and honeysuckle

There's superradiance

in the motion of clouds — concepts spinning
particles unseen
and falling, dark matter's
steady hum —

she lives in memory
now, communes with cirrocumulus — today
less real than yesterday's
still-stirring fires —

the gentling
strum of classical guitars, light and shadow
in her palms, her heart —

night turns time on its head
masks the ending
so there was no fall
no darkling core
just lake-cliffs' crumbled
face —

Perhaps we need a different discernment
black holes where God
divides —

to glide, planes-of-motion low to the ice
friction gone

Inspire

Her voice like a river —
some days overflowing,   others parched
ox-bow silted,   trapped —
waiting for storm-surge,   hurricane's land-fall
seas at high tide

During dry spells,   she would
suck air into her lungs,   hold for five,   expel
repeat,   transcending tension,   bronchioles
to alveoli —   lungs' costal surface
visceral

like those incised meanders
along a river's lower course —   erosion's
outside bend   seeking rejuvenation —   knick-
points and waterfalls   breaking
turbulent

Taking Breath

It’s all in the scale —
curves conceived & winding, warping
emptiness —
fractal lines self-
similar & infinite

Our lava secrets’ crusted
core embedded deep in magma’s
viscous creep —
a confluence
of faults, their push-and-pull
beyond earth’s dark
rendering

This universe
our own eyes see —
truths singular & metaphoric

mere intervals — our in-between-
ness breathing

Some Might Say It's Kismet

Transcending solitudes —   crossed threads
& contradictions,   delicately
stitched —

A referendum rejecting separation —
coincidence
          serendipity and
                    je ne sais quoi —

overtures,   an invitation,   space-time's
weave —

curious laws and probabilities
a quantum
of deeper truth   that keeps us
          from unravelling

Contours of Possession

...things that I do
in the dark
reaching for you
whoever you are
— June Jordan

That curving space between
what's real,   what
isn't —   erasure's whittling
& *things I do*   *in the dark*

Where breadth and density
colour voice,   blur
melody's subtle shift —
rhythmic layers
reciprocity's

loops,   the lyric "I"
invisible & intimate —   as meaning's
steep
terrain un / folds   *reaching for you*
whoever you are

Yes, Just So

I must learn the contours of your face —
move fingers knowingly
across each feature —
your eyes, cheekbone's line
the texture of your lips
your brow

There can be no mistaking — your face
or mine
whose turn it is to touch —

small circular movements smoothing
clay, our lines
of symmetry —

spend more time there …

Yes, just so

More Than Meets the Eye

Was it nostalgia,   the instability
of green —   translucent bone-
leaf   latticed,   radiant
an excitation   illumining dark's
tender,   sculpted
intervals —

pure-blue tones,   lavender amber-warm
& gently lit —   languorous
as breath
truth's
lumen space
among the shadows —
honeycombed

What (we think) We Know —

memories'
mingled dreams, the *why* of syntax braced
& intimate —
landing in this place, the selvage-
edge unravelling —

crumpling's creases, messy
& irregular —
truth un-laundered, & shallow's sudden leap
to deep —
in pen's *ink-damp*
immediacy

words' lingering hunger, & questions
filleting the heart

In Love and Books

Assurance fades
like ink between endpapers —
almost-and-already hidden
texts & simulacra
          awaiting affirmation —

each folio
                    a witness
leaf-secured,   tipped-
in,   the binding edge   whip-stitched —
          almost   perfect —

                                        Along the folds
every passing thread   a penetration —   length
of spine,   hinge
on which we
swing —

kettle-stitches locked,   grooves
notched & milled —
bonding sometimes,   *dos-à-dos*
          & opposite —

mindful   of warp & mulberry
          mending tears

No Soft Return

She was drawn to swamps,   naked
trees   resisting
Spring

wakes to shades of morning   stretched
across the ceiling,   angling walls
          like parallel protractors

a tunnel of trees,   an underpass
then sunlight —
between windows' span,   blinds
          wide-shuttered

Where was she   the day the cliffs
gave way —
released their tenuous hold
on clay —   a primal rush of cloud
          piercing the bay

landscape's seismic   shift
between them —   shadow-selves
& thunder
          knit to bone

The Past as Prologue

Tenacious as a vine —   invasive
roots relentless,   tendrils
                                        poised —
years long-gone   can surface,   tensile
          newly-angled

She thought them put to rest —
that book,   those poems,   autumn's
                                        pruning
yet there they were —   like rioting green-
dark leaves   netting the weathered fence
each morning —   outlasting cedars
          intentions crystalline

Today,   a chipmunk scurried
across the lawn   unmoved by vines
lilies-of-the-valley,   delphinium's
thick thatch,   bishop's
evergreen

Soon,   she must devise
new canticles & lamentations,   dig
deep for rhizomes
construct a bier —   this time
leave not the smallest
shred

Third Person Baroque

i.

Remembrance sits between us —
a third person, silent
brooding like a bruise —

beyond our window, a symphony
of trees plays golden
notes, each leaf and stem
attuned —

autumn's baroque sensibilities
ruby-tinged
red —
honeyed heartwood
echoing

ii.
I wore your cooling fragrance
like a stole
blessing jasmine's silence —
petals woven
stems twined, as slender fingers
reached
across the sand —

your presence sharp, a sweet
implosion
on the tongue

Finding Her Bearings

She's discerning   clearly now
each moment's promise   cutting,   razor-sharp —

poems   not an end,   but skin
sensors   of soft touch

There were days   she'd keep an eye
on the passing parade
now,   this aging space
where each name   is an invocation —
a house in which they danced,   sutured wounds
made a home —

scattering violets and blues,   beyond
Sun's darkening

Flaunting

In their home's private spaces,
a thousand caring declarations
          year-over-year-

over-year —   Now she wants
to brandish a flag,   design a decal
affix it
          to the back bumper

          Like *Hooker & Sons*
attached to her two-tone,   metallic-
burgundy   *Oldsmobile Cutlass Salon 442* —
its flaunting sport console,   bucket seats
          & contoured insinuations

          Like racing stripes
streaked wide along the sides —   distinctive
                    rocker-
          panels,   lower doors,   wheel-
wells   & that emblematic 442 —   its large
font marking her
          path across the city

All the while,   longing
to proclaim:

watch these wheels —   watch how
          we hug   a curve

Divining

Think of it more
as derring-do —
dials on the panel easy to read at first
later, more gut and reflex —
when to choose
straight climbs
descend, let go
stay level —

split-seconds
sometimes, grasping
myriad cues, reach of maps —
those inevitable gaps
in our carefully constructed frames —
divining what we
do

Against All Odds

we've shared twelve thousand days and more
weathered ice-storms,   power failures,   several
cats,   re-negotiated mortgages and joy
        love's fierce trajectories —
equal parts laughter,   sadness,   subtle alchemies

lately,   I've been dreaming grassy pools
moist sand,   birds   the colours of crushed coral —
fragile,   thin-boned,   soft —
        perhaps a snowy egret,   plovers
or sandpipers   rumpled white —   no sense

of why —   they seemed deliberate
induced by cinnamon,   lemon,   or stevia
shaken well —   three sprays
under the tongue —   the murmur of nuns
        poems,   promises and paths

while all I ask   are breath and you —   to find my
way through fog and wilderness —   to walk
        on water,   lightly

II: Umbra

Sometimes

a single step
is one too many — warnings missed
plateaus, the ultimate constraint —
eggshells' paved asymmetry
transgressive
as breathing

Time to tune the poem
let its pitch course through —
lay bearings
hitch-pins
mindful
of intervals, melody's perfectly imperfect
cresting — infinity slowly
loosening the strings

Je ne regrette …

(with a nod to Piaf)

They shared warm rolls,   a touch of chives
                        & sweetness —
Spring's early rain-freeze
on Cathedral Bluffs
                    groynes' broken
                                  waves —
an ancient glacier's   cut-and-drift beyond
      the gully —

lake's slow rotation,   a sunken ship's
                          rusted hull
      night's unravelling —

Their lives,   a question of shear,   or merely
milkweed seeds   dispersing white
      -on-wind

Implausible

When matter & antimatter
met,   they should have cancelled
                    each other
yet here they are —   oscillating
          even now

As Hadron's magnets release
                  their grip
on gamma rays,   crystal scintillations
& beauty's implausible
          flicker

particles play tag
& ask:
Who watches
        the watchman?

On deciphering

i.

the peculiar physics
of crumpling — rumpled pages
devoid of memory

an early snowfall of singular stillness —
the way an insect's wing un-
furls — inertia
wind-drag
torque

ii.
dawn's promise
like uncertainty's butterfly —
flexing its wings

our topography of scars
their tensile-
strength revealed

Magnus Effect

for Chantal

i.

Consider the knuckleball
its lift and drag —
fingertips and air over seam — paths that flutter-
dance or curve:
butterflies in flight — *if it's high*
let it fly

takes skill to master, and to catch — best to wait
till it stops
rolling — always trade-offs — *let it go*
if it's low

That critical velocity when a sphere's in flow, sweet-
spot let loose

ii.

This is where you
summon topspin,   gravity's pull —   its thrust
and torque —
where slow pays off   in cut & curve —
a perfect aim

Cricket's red-leather backspin   skidding
off the pitch —
a batter's love-lofted pull   to the long-on rope
two square drives
caressed

Or maybe you just want
to bowl them out,   leg-before-wicket —
deliver that wicked,   under-
handed   throw

No Reversals

She pads a calico path,   silent
on rain-soaked leaves

sidewalks,   muffled-bronze
asphalt slick   with damp November

Trees bear witness
on this stately   house-lined street

oak and ash
red maple,   willows weeping

A discerning cat
knows   what the sign decrees —

no reversals
on this One-Way street

Beyond Sun's Reach

i.
Observe the light
take note of hours,   shade's dark
inclination —

dappled or deep,   filtered through leaf
or buried beneath canopies —   those under-
story mosses,   lichens,   grass,   impatient
        ferns & lilies

                                        of-the-valley —
partial shade's contrasting
greens,   where hellebore's baneful beauty
& hostas thrive   beyond sun's
                                    reach

We name them: viola,   pansy,   anemone
        heartsease —

our words eclipsing   luna's dusky-
rose & moon's silvered grace —
as obscurity reveals its charms   in umbra's
        defiant flourishing

ii.
Attend to mulching,   weeding
                                        pregnant nouns —
boxwood replaced
                                by mulberry —
flowers' muted palettes,   pampas grass
        & feathered inflorescence

                        mindful
of the understory,   careful pruning
                                old-wood scars —
where even hydrangeas   are known
        to bloom

iii.
When drought occurs,   remember
        Rule and *Sarton*
surreptitious brown-bagged books —
artful texts,   & words
                                embedded —
enduring blossoms,   rejecting
        sculptural seed

Umbra

Some days we sit in earth's dark
limb, life's ruddy glow
refracted, sunlit-red —
super-flower blood-moons
eclipsing the horizon

uncertainties skim just
inside the umbra, sensed
yet still to be
revealed —

no wrong turns, just those un-
expected paths and invitations
in totality's low-hanging
orb

Starlight's Wind

Here on Sagan's pale blue dot
our lives play
like interstellar specks
across the sky —
tenuous as light-sail luminosity
starlight's wind

subjectivities messy & irregular
sometimes
whimsical, mirror the imagined
& the real —

diaphanous as dust suspended
in a sunbeam —
scattering sun's true
un / filtered light

Bewildering Reveals

Between Earth,   and Moon's
slivered darkness,   we search for life's elemental
broth —
its once-invisible light,   hours tuned
to nothingness —
elegant equations   attempting to resolve
the question:
Could we melt away   for good?

Maybe we're approaching boundary's
verge —
where we can't understand,   can't afford
an answer
to breath's fleeting tide-spin
those deeper conundrums: *Might the universe*
have a guiding hand?

As floodwaters rise   and fractures form
attribution's errors
reach out
claw back
spreading   like ink-pools—

Broken Symmetries

This universe of byways & enigmas
paths to wisdom
                        inside-outside-
in —   spontaneous
as that fourth charmed quark
beyond up,   down
& strange —

kaons switching back & forth
like poets of the void
                        confronting quiet
urgencies —   days' dark intervals
their broken
                symmetries

Windows of Alignment

See irises and lilacs
                    blooming yearly
on new growth —   the eastern phoebe
spring's first songbird,   setting her course
by stars,   the sun,   & Earth's
          magnetic field —

She boasts no wing-bars
no special warble-music —
just fidelity's   unerring bond
to culvert,   bridge,   or barn —

never tempted to digress
from nesting's yearly moss
          & leaves

Alert to coasts & mountains
landscape's odour —
yearning perhaps   for windows
of alignment   eclipsing
          moons —

beyond milkweed's   clay-wet loam
        bee-balm,   & butterflies

Orange among the Rocks

Smooth as a muted sax   and barely
                    audible
truth's naked moments   sidle up to text
strive for different
geometries —

an oyster-catcher
its long-curved beak   sings orange
among the rocks —
sea and weeds   misconstrued
among a fluency of ferns
moist
from constant rain

Melancholy music,   pure
as sine waves,   measures sun's true
declination,   traces lines
like braille

as twilight slants   along the frieze
and pine resin bleeds
        its moss-green light

Refractions from the 38th Floor

— Harbour Castle Weston

A summer evening's slow
maneuvering —
sailboats sculpt graceful liquid-
loops —
water-taxis bob & weave
between the ferries — lake skin
ruffled velvet

CN Tower's brooding chairoscuro lengthens
leisurely
sun moves West —
glare's too great to capture ripples'
trailing light —
to see
through lovers' eyes, lens-refracted —
bending brokenness
its deep-green heart

Through the Narrows

— Halifax Harbour

Floating docks   rise
                    & fall
in ferries' silken wake —
the *Harbour Queen,*   the *Rita Joe* —
& water's surface   shaded
          turquoise

Three long-winged gulls
& a naval helicopter   calculate wind-
                    drift —
wailing-calls   & rotors' blade-
slap   spinning
          Cyclone-grey

As we head for open water
consider tidal volumes,   coastal
breathing —
               a hole in the sea
a rogue wave —   troughs
leaving us
          guileless
in shimmer's reflection —

sounding depths
          to plumb the heart

III: Working the Margins

Some poems

arrive casually
drop by —
mere acquaintances,   they grow
on you,   occupy corners
of your mind
till you succumb
to text
get serious —

then,   never-ending pruning,   fine-
tuning —   density's weight
in edge and line
anchoring dream's fluid evocation —

an endless journey towards equivalence —
poem's holy grail

No Such Thing

What if all books were already part-written
each beyond a second draft —
authors convinced   they're starting
from scratch —

(there's no such thing)

beginnings scroll back,   maybe light years —
narrative threads   to discern
lines   to break —

the middle
where the action really is
unravelling —

like new-found worlds   transiting
their mother star
pin-points barely glimpsed

our words' raw steel,   smoky-grey
& smouldering

The Aftermath

The moon was wet
a pool of silver haze —
night's Payne's grey canvas   light-sensitive
and blurring —

Yet   there was a sharpness
to the dark,   an urgency that seemed
to burn —
perhaps a bruise   palpable,   soft
pooling tender

She mused about walls,   identity's
layers & cross-hairs —
malleable enclosures   shimmering *yes*
summoning *no* —
erasures   harvesting surrender —
what can & cannot be

Paths travelled,   clearer now,   colour
her voice   electric-blue

Its Raw-Unknowing

Poems lower rope-lines
down well's echoing shaft —
each a frond   as yet
                  unfurled

language nascent in its raw-
unknowing —

Sometimes it breaks
                  embraces uncertainty —
where to place a syllable,   caesura
— long dash
loses its bearings
in the universe

The page,   a dark-water-
pool   beneath stands of cedars
                  new-growth   verging —
ragged shadows releasing
errant light —

while mind's imperfect waterfall
plunges over bedrock
                  erodes fault lines
          traces the unsaid

Where She Stands

Perhaps it's time
to cast a net,   troll words
release the minnows —
careful to preserve   quiet
urgencies —
a phrase,   a stolen river,   water's
shifting reach

pressure
on the clutch —
the whine-and-screech
first-to-second-to-
third,   then back —   no time
          for fourth.   Each

restless surge
in life's too-sharp
manoeuvres —   ill-timed
          & misaligned

On Pivot's Edge

Her mother lived fiercely
                    never left a bridge
un / burned,   or at least   destabilized —
a beam   a burr
          a cantilevered arch —
even a subtle insinuation   would
                    suffice

While she   bent backwards to keep
          a truss in place
learned   to step over obstacles
                    assume the perfect tandem-
balance —
eyes closed,   arms outstretched
mindful   of lacunar's bleed —

          and the load
                    each bridge   might bear

En Route

Cushioned in the after-glow
of reading's affirmation,   she conjures
scenarios —

lemon-slivers in our drinks,   a subtle
sense of speed   and wind-rush
cabin pressure
holding —

angels,   lost madonnas   cleaving
night sky
a pyroclastic river   breathing
ash

Beyond the Boeing's narrow aisle
satellites track   moon's tether

friends and lovers wait
weigh
probabilities —

wine-red,   and measured

Reprise

Across the Plains of Abraham,   light
                                        lingers
on river's darkening —
Venus rises slowly   in evening's
wintry sky

Beyond our window's panoramic sweep
a grey haze   settles the river —
the far shore,   a mere
        insinuation

Joy drips through   like a dark-
roast   filter-fine —
scores gentle licks   with tip
and tongue —
parry & riposte,   feint
                                & flèche
        catching the tempo

And when it's right —
        reprise

Takin' Stock

Swaying each morning
to Country,   memory's muscle
rockin'
          steady —

those hurtin' songs'   slow
deep chords   strumming
every nerve —   cadence
          broken

As we value fluctuation
the vagaries of tides —
                                        amortize
and hold for long-term
          yield —

where symmetry's balance
can   be overrated
and even the heart
                                        skews

After the Elizabeth Bishop Symposium

— Halifax, N.S.

It's Sunday,   the morn anointed,   warm
                                        with salt —
beyond Duncan's Cove,   a lone steamer
          breaches   the horizon

We feast on cornbread,   cheese and lemon-
                                        crescent moons
collected works,   lonely gospels
a liturgy of loss —
fine lines   thinly-sliced   between reticence
                                        and revelation
          where virtue lies in metaphor —

clouds' patchwork quilt,   the red-tinged fog
          enhancing ocean's ragged
                    choreography

Ecology of Days

Above the inland sea
an aging inn — lake-view windows streaked
with morning —
shoreline's shattered ice sharply-slivered

a broken bay, open water
cold fronts holding

Steeped
in a wet and slow ecology of days, she toys
with green — thoughts
of warm bread, a chilled *Corona,* rice
with black beans —

weighs the distance
to make it there — that shimmering
space of cobalt blues, unencumbered
certain of passage —
the unequivocal break-up
of spring ice

Framed Silences

Certain memories are rounded
water-worn like cobblestone,   others granite-
chiseled
each piece evocative —

a copper etching,   tall ships
Moroccan vendor's purpled aubergines,   wooden crates
flooded green —
watercolour-sidewalks,   and indigo archways
fading

fleeting strokes   solar-gold
infuse a wall —   while ladybugs play   amid
a wild banana's verdant
flowering

Framed silences
proclaiming provenance
others,   incognito —
as we cull artifacts
our unexamined archives,   dislodged
& crumbling —

pebbles pounded into sand,   loose crushed stones —
rills & runoffs
streaming

Spilling Her Wild

The way a day can slip out of your hand,
your senses spill like water
— Dionne Brand, *Thirsty*

i.

Some recollections surface   satin-soft
beneath the skin: a winter's night
late dinner   breaching
that fine line —
a project's passion   deeply-
held   & passion
          pure and simple

the question:
          So what do-you-think?
probing storm's inside
eye —
                              a fulcrum
more like ocean,   more dream
its freighted liability
dances through
                         weathers

the looming span
of years —

ii.
Numbers she might have called
long out-of-service —   then obituary's
          chance view:
humanitarian,   *gifted artist's*
          peaceful passing
no next of kin,   no named
                                        loved one
          left to mourn

memories   spilling —
her wild,   transgressive absence

          grieved

Against the Grain

As rivulets of slanting rain
streak
the windows — beaded drops, tadpole tails
damp with flailing

she conjures Royal Poincianas
feels her way through powers, principalities
& thunderstorms —
a tropical depression between Bahamas and Cuba

locutionary acts, & night's accidental insights
diaphanous, unfettered, crystal-
pure — floating
free

On Letting Go

Measure turbulence,   friction's
force —
remembrance a river,   a confluence of
                                        tides —
bed-shear's hungry water,   braiding
        & re-braiding

those sinuous meanders   & long slow curves
                                        arc's
bend —   abrasion's scars asserting
once-&-for-all,   no such thing as

        All under the bridge

Fluid Residues

Lest the brain forget the thunder
The roused heart once made it hear
— Louise Bogan, *The Blue Estuaries*

Perhaps it was the lightning's   jagged path
                                        ions pooled
soft hail,   and droplets
super-cooled —

skeletons of cloud suspending sky
rappelling
        mountains —

those quicker,   shorter turns
between the gates
                                        vertical
                                        drops
ski-tips shining

Lawns mowed in ribbon-strips
                                        of green
energy's dynamic gestures,   a roused
heart's
        thunder

as nostalgia's fluid residue works
the margins —

acuities   that age acquires
                                marking

        the unsaid

IV: Hypotheticals

Playing with God

Wandering the wilderness
between *no more*
and then *not yet*
ashes trailing
she strains to hear the music —
its redemptive narrative

keeps watch for fallacies —
those shadowed remnants & fabrications
coming together, then slipping
apart —

while choirs of angels wait in their wings
attentive
to false notes

Hypotheticals

Surely there's
time enough for conjuring moons
celestial bodies, boundless
yearning —
time enough
for coral's deep and breathless beauty
dashes of gold
and black's rough glaze

To hold the text
in your hand, receive the words —
those irreversible truths
too late discerned — stones' silent
presence — the peal
of stillness

slipping away without a trace, hours
lengthening
to absence — as if you never
had been there

Too Soon

Sheets of rain's early freeze
                    strafe   the lake —
obscure its blinding-silver
undulations

Autumn's dying bluster,   constant
                              & unyielding as
memory's accreting
silt —   mercy's prayer   a solar flare
                              molten-red
rupturing night's membrane
          like a semaphore

          Our minds battling long
between the abstract & hard truths
                              too soon eclipsed —
vein's ragged bleeding
          incandescent-blue

When nearly everything's

left unsaid
particulars fade away —
that sweep of windows above
St. John's harbour, vodka on-the-
rocks, & her notebook
capturing the feel
of solitude
its precise geometry —

like "Orion's Bar," where solar systems'
hot young stars bob-and-weave
beyond the reach of ultra-
violet, nebula's
crisp dark —

enough for strokes though — finite
& countable —
a Saturday-night watering hole
tendering
destiny's
ischemic touch

Harbouring Certainties

From the Courtyard Marriott, St. John's

This evening
there were outages —
(no one knows why)
She sips Portuguese Port — been told
a Newfoundland connection's
guaranteed —

her gaze on low-lying hills slope-rough
and weathered
The Narrows' channeled mouth — its ancient
fjord's ridge

Wisps of mist roll in — as foghorns'
mournful warnings
echo
and the *Atlantic Osprey* glides ghostlike
towards the dock

Perhaps tomorrow moist-green hills —
power's hard return

Her Corona Radiata Already Knows

i.

That Sunday morning in St. John's
its sudden   dis /articulated
veering —

focus to ~ *out of* ~   *steady* ~ to *un* ~

a blurring zag
a yawing depth-
of-field —

She gropes for shoes,   her cell phone
purse
door's   double-
latch

Calls reception —

Mercy's intersecting orbits intertwined
& tilting —

Duckworth   to Le Marchand
Marriott
to St. Clare's

Past noon,   & she's already altered
course —
the poets' conference ending soon —
where she will not
be
reading

ii.
Deep-brain arteries   so small,   it takes
real effort for a
clot   to plot its
path —

then   three days
before diffusion-weighted imaging confirms
what her corona radiata
        already knows —
                a left thalamic infarct
                        lacunar
                acute
        & irreversible

Frenzy-feeding

                              Beyond her hospital window
humpback hills   sprawl weather-worn
                              & scruffy —
in coves & bays,   capelin
are roiling —

shoals of small fish   silver-sweeping
                              onto shore —
males with spawning ridges,   females
delicate & smooth
bearing roe —
seabirds,   gulls,   & frenzy-feeding
                                        seals
rise   with the tide

                              Tonight,   she harbours
thoughts of dinner —   shepherd's pie
soup's country vegetables,   apple juice
                                        jello's
orange moments —

savours the singular kindness
of strangers —
the grainy textures
          of stewed pears —

Ephemera

The way thought
                    echoes —
open seas
acts of invocation
illusory as time's accidental narratives
                    poem-bones and risk —
finicky particulars between thumb
and finger,   like coastlines
threading
          thought

Desire's guarded eloquence,   joy's
manoeuvering
                    then loss —
          us   we   you
mere parentheses   enclosing
                                        silence —

          (as) memory   breaks

Impromptu

Our lives play out   in open-
          ended fragments —
phrases captured on the fly
culled,   curated
                    twilled
spinning silk   from dross

impromptu's dusky measures,   achingly
                                        exuberant
dark   as Titan-seas —
mournful,   restless melodies
minor-keyed
          codas trailing

articulation's broken chords
in 3/4 time,   leaning
          into the curve

Undeterred

As scientists brace for glimpses —
a super-Earth,   a Sun-like star orbiting
so near   that oceans boil —
a hemisphere in searing light,   another
        endless dark

she reads of hoary mountain mint
lavender-heads   abuzz
with bees & lazy waterlily-
leaves —

counts on antivirals,   a nurse's early-
morning call —   embraces
uncertainty's perfectly   measured
sentences

while pandemic clouds rain ash
& swallows
        dive —

On Betting Against Perpetuities

There are no rules for constancy,   homeo
stasis,   what life does —

the palpable realities of silence   unheard
& marginal —

a temperamental reticence,   gaps & lost
years —   memory's

incantatory burden,   lightning
sealed in glass —

reconciliations shifting,   alchemical
& intimate —   dissolving

            what defines us

Death plucked a feather

from her wing —
          held it in trust

barbs beneath
the down —   afterfeathers,   hollow
          shaft,   a quill —
an eye all-seeing
luminescent   as a peacock's
hurl & flue

I reached for it —
keep it on my person   as assurance
                                        I am learning
how to bear it lightly —
          its subtle energy
                    radiant lift

Time's Tilt

i.
Ephemeral moments   when
anything is possible—
casters tilting
as the wheel steers —
          then camber,   the angle
of wear
eroding our hearts

ii.
Not just
having a mind,   but
the art of entering —
the way one page
          presses up against the next
& the universe expands
in a blink —

each day,   a waiting-room
one window only,   transcending
time & truth —
          nothing absolute
                    nothing permanent —
just thought's thin haze
impossible
to hold

Of one thing

I can be certain —

the next totality
will not find me at our kitchen table watching
its shadow curve
patio stones,   then spring's newly-
wakened lawn
as outdoor lights respond to dark
in moon's swift
embrace

Perhaps I'll have another hard-
return   as someone
else —
atoning still
for lives
lived

a barely-discernable cosmic
flicker —
revelling
in paradox & serendipity

yearning
for more

Notes

In the art

The study of a viscous incompressible fluid 's flow through a compliant tube has many applications. One major application is blood flow through human arteries.

I: Subtle Alchemies

Sight-lines

hook and tumble is from Mary Oliver's comment on first meeting her lifelong partner, photographer, Molly Malone: "I took one look and fell, hook and tumble."

There's superradiance

Influenced by: "Waterloo Meeting Offers Fresh Spin on Black Holes" by Ivan Semeniuk, *The Globe and Mail*, May 12, 2018; and "A Very Different Next Act," Robert Everett-Green's article on Tessa Virtue and Scott Moir discussing the challenge of putting dance forms on ice, in *The Globe and Mail*, May 10, 2018.

black holes,   where God divides is from the lines: "*Black holes are where/ God divides by zero*" from Alice Major's poem "Zero Divided by Zero," in *Welcome to the Anthropocene* (2018).

Contours of Possession

Variation on a glosa, after reading "These Poems" from *Directed by Desire: The Collected Poems of June Jordan* (2005); and Emily Donaldson's review of Doireann Ní Ghriola*'s A Ghost in the Throat* (2021), *The Globe and Mail*, July 17, 2021.

Yes,   Just So

The poem echoes sculptors Frances Loring and Florence Wyle, who were lifelong partners. They shared three studio homes over the years. At their first home, in New York's Greenwich Village in the early 1900s, they sculpted well-known portrait busts of each other. These evocative pieces are now in the Loring-Wyle Parkette, at St. Clair Avenue and Mount Pleasant Road, in Toronto.

More Than Meets the Eye

After viewing a reading of *Lighting Martha, A One-Act Play about Jean Rosenthal*, by Carolyn Gage, 2018.

What (we think) We Know —

Reference to *crumpling* is from Siobhan Robert's article "The Latest Wrinkle in Crumple Theory;" the image *ink-damp/ immediacy* is from "Her Secret Selves," Megan O'Grady's review of *The Copenhagen Trilogy, Childhood, Youth, Dependency* (2021) by Tove Ditlevsen; both published in *The New York Times Book Review*, February 20-21, 2021.

Taking Breath

Found poem starting with i) "The Truth is out there," a review by Ivan Semeniuk of James Peebles' "The Whole Truth: A Cosmologist's Reflections on the Search for Objective Reality" in *The Globe and Mail*, August 13, 2022; and ii) "Lava Samples Reveal Secrets of a Volcano" by Oliver Whang, in the *New York Times International Weekly, The Toronto Star,* August 6-7, 2022.

Finding Her Bearings

The italicized lines are from notes I made during a talk by A. F. Moritz at the League of Canadian Poets AGM/ Conference, Toronto, June, 2017.

II. Umbra

Je ne regrette ...

Title is a nod to Édith Piaf's iconic song, "Je ne regrette rien." "Cathedral Bluffs" is the name given to a part of Toronto's Scarborough Bluffs. Groynes are barriers, such as those large armour stones installed along the shore of the Scarborough Bluffs to break the force of the waves from Lake Ontario and slow down erosion.

Implausible

Informed by "Intermission for the Biggest Machine Ever" by Dennis Overbye, *The New York Times International Weekly*, in the *Toronto Star*, January 5-6, 2019. "Hadron" refers to the Large Hadron Collider, located in Switzerland.

On deciphering

Informed by "This is the Way the Paper Crumples" by Siobhan Roberts, *The Toronto Star*, January 6, 2019. The phrase "the peculiar physics/ of crumpling" is a variation on the title, "Scrunch Time: The Peculiar Physics of Crumpled Paper," *New Scientist*, December 20, 2011.

Magnus Effect

The Magnus effect is a lift force of tremendous importance to athletes who want to bend the flight of a ball. It causes the curved flight of balls that are thrown, hit or kicked, and at the same time are given a spin. Leg before wicket (LBW) is a term in cricket. When the ball strikes any part of the batter's body (not necessarily the leg), and, in the *umpire's* judgement, the ball would have hit the batter's stumps but for this interception, then the batter is out.

Beyond Sun's Reach

Influenced by the article "Death Becomes Them" by Adrienne Matei, *The Globe and Mail*, *Style Advisor*, April 17, 2020, pp. 42-43. "Understory" refers to the underlying layers of vegetation in a forest. The italicized names refer to writers May Sarton and Jane Rule. The image "sculptural seed" is from a line in Matei's article: "A thatch of flowers gone to sculptural seed."

Umbra

After "West Coast Skywatchers Will Get Best View of Wednesday's Total Lunar Eclipse," by Ivan Semeniuk, *The Globe and Mail*, May 25, 2021.

Starlight's Wind

Starting with the article "Aliens Must Be Out There," by Farhad Manjoo, *The New York Times International Weekly*, February 20-21, 2021. And the quote: "We live aboard astronomer Carl Sagan's pale blue dot, 'a mote of dust suspended in a sunbeam.'"

Bewildering Reveals

After *The Globe and Mail* editorial "A Telescope to Answer: Are We Alone," Thursday, December 30, 2021; the article, "Working in Harmony with Earth Beneath" by Siddhartha Mitter, *The New York Times International Weekly*, December 11-12, 2021; and the obituary for psychologist Lee Ross,

"Stanford Professor was Expert in Why We Misunderstand Each Other," by Alex Traub, *The Globe and Mail*, June 21, 2021.

Broken Symmetries

A quark is the smallest particle (unit of matter) in the universe. There are six flavours of quarks: up, down, strange, charmed, bottom and top. A kaon is a particle made of one up quark or down quark, and one strange quark.

Windows of Alignment

Information on the eastern phoebe from Marcus Gee's article "How a Dull Little Bird Brightened a Dismal Year," *The Globe and Mail*, May 29, 2021.

Orange Among the Rocks

A sine wave is the simplest model of a musical sound, according to Mathematical Harmonies, by Mark Petersen, https://amath.colorado.edu/pub/matlab/music/MathMusic.pdf. "Sine is a natural sway, the epitome of smoothness" from "Intuitive Understanding of Sine Waves," https://betterexplained.com/articles/intuitive-understanding-of-sine-waves/. "Declination" refers to the angle of the sun at any given time.

III: Working the Margins

No Such Thing

Dream sequence influenced by NASA's 2017 report on the discovery of dwarf star Trappist-1 and its seven orbiting planets, summarized in: "Keeping Seven Worlds from Colliding," by Kenneth Chang, *New York Times International Weekly*, May 27-28, 2017. And the article "A Real Metal Head: How Steel Decor Reflects Life's Imperfections," on interior and furniture designer Francoise Turner-Larcade, by Matthew Hague, *The Globe and Mail*, September 22, 2016.

En Route

A pyroclastic flow is a mixture of volcanic fragments travelling along the ground away from a volcanic vent. These flows can be deadly because of their high temperature and mobility.

Reprise

The terms "parry & riposte, feint & flèche" are fencing moves.

Spilling Her Wild

Epigraph from "XXVIII," by Dionne Brand, *Thirsty*, McClelland & Stewart, 2002, p. 52.

Fluid Residues

Epigraph from "Sub Contra," by Louise Bogan, *The Blue Estuaries, 1923-1968*, The Ecco Press, N.Y., 1977 (4th Printing, 1985), p. 5, lines 6-7.

IV: Hypotheticals

Playing with God

Variations on a found poem influenced by "Stripping the Novel Down to Its Frame," Jenny Offill's review of *Kudos* by Rachel Cusk, *The New York Times Book Review*, June 23-24, 2018.

Title influenced by Richard Russo's advice to novelists: "If playing God scares you, there are other professions," quoted in "Nobody's Fool," Jay Fielden's review of Richard Russo's *The Destiny Thief, Essays on Writing, Writers and Life*, *The New York Times Book Review*, Ibid., p. 8.

When nearly everything's

Ischemic is a medical term which means that an organ (e.g. the brain, heart, etc.) is not getting enough blood or oxygen.

Her Corona Radiata Already Knows

The corona radiata connects motor and sensory nerve pathways in the brain. A thalamic stroke is a type of lacunar stroke that takes place in a deep part of the brain. The thalamus is involved in many crucial aspects of everyday life including speech, memory, balance, motivation, and sensations of physical touch and pain.

Ephemera

Influenced by my notes from the Elizabeth Bishop Symposium, *"It Must be Nova Scotia": Negotiating Place in the Writings of Elizabeth Bishop*, Halifax, June 9-12, 2011.

Impromptu

Titan is one of Saturn's moons.

Death plucked a feather

"Hurl" feathers are very fine and featherly, e.g. from a peacock's tail. The largest part of a feather is the plume (a shaft with branched barbs and barbules). A single barb with barbules is called a "plumule." All the plumules together form the "flue."

Time's Tilt

Influenced by "The Sense of an Ending," Denis Overbye's review of *Until the End of Time, Mind, Matter and Our Search for Meaning in an Evolving Universe*, by Brian Greene, *New York Times Book Review*, March 14-15, 2020. The lines "the way one page/ presses up against the next" and "each day a waiting-room/ one window only" are variations on lines from Emma Donoghue's *Learned by Heart* (2023): "the way one page presses itself against the next." (p. 306); and "the present is a waiting-room with only one window, facing back" (p. 301).

Of one thing

On April 8, 2024, a total solar eclipse moved across North America, passing over Mexico, the United States, and Canada. A total solar eclipse happens when the Moon passes between the Sun and Earth, completely blocking the face of the Sun. The sky will darken as if it were dawn or dusk. The next total solar eclipse to be visible in Canada will occur on August 22, 2044.

Acknowledgments

My thanks to poet Allan Briesmaster, Aeolus House publisher, for his thoughtful editing and support for my work, to Julie McNeill for designing a beautiful book, and to John Oughton for his early proofreading and editorial input. Much appreciation to visual artist Judith Davidson-Palmer for the striking photograph that graces the cover.

To the poets of the Long Dash group: Elana Wolff, John Oughton, Sheila Stewart, Kath McLean, Merle Nudelman, Clara Blackwood and Brenda Clews, my appreciation for their insightful feedback and ongoing friendship. This book would not have been possible without their unfailing encouragement, especially in my early stroke-recovery years.

Thanks to the Editors of the publications in which earlier versions of the following poems appeared: "There's Superradiance," *Vallum,* 16:1, *Connections,* 2019, p. 17; and "Against All Odds," *The Maynard*, Spring, 2019.

Special appreciation to the League of Canadian Poets' staff, members of the Executive and poets who were there for me in St. John's when I most needed support, and to the Manager of the Courtyard Marriott and her staff for their many kindnesses.

My deepest gratitude, as always, to my partner of many years, Anne-Marie Caron-Reaume, for her caring presence & constant affirmation. This book is for her.

About the Author

Photo: J. Davidson-Palmer

Mary Lou Soutar-Hynes is a Jamaican-Canadian poet/educator and former nun. She's the author of four collections of poetry: *Any Waking Morning* (2019), *Dark Water Songs* (2013), *Travelling Light* (2006), long-listed for the 2007 ReLit Poetry Award, and *The Fires of Naming* (2001). Her work reflects her interest in ekphrastic poetry, poetic inquiry, and more recently, science as poetic inspiration. She has been published in Canada, the UK, and the Netherlands. Her work includes poetry and essays in journals and anthologies, and chapters in edited books. A member of The League of Canadian Poets and The Writers' Union of Canada, she was a Fellow at Scotland's Hawthornden International Retreat for Writers in 2009, and is an alumna of the 1998 Banff Writing Studio Program. Retired from the Ontario Ministry of Education, she lives and writes in Toronto.

Other Recent Aeolus House Books

Four-Square Poems by James Deahl
Life, after life – from epitaph to epilogue by A. Garnett Weiss
Scar Atlas by Colin Morton
COVID-19 Blues by Barbara Landry
Stronger in Broken Places by John B. Lee
Motion Over Time by Elaine Batcher
A Balance Between Sorrows by Dorothy Sandler-Glick
In the Spaces Between Bonsai by Terry Ann Carter
Homeless City by Donna Langevin and Kate Rogers
Holding Close by Carolyn Taylor
DiVERSity by Margaret Code
The Black Ship by David Clink
Another Open Door by Ann Elizabeth Carson
So That We Might Finger the Words by Sue Chenette
Consider by Susan McCaslin
Everchild by Gwynn Scheltema
Rain on My Skin by Rosemary Clewes
Learning To Leave by Ariane Blackman
To Grace Bridges by Thomas Gannon Hamilton
Digging by Kate Marshall Flaherty
The Fragmentarium and Other Poems by Chris Pannell
Wet Toes by Mary Nyquist
Loose Ends by Ann Elizabeth Carson
The Many Faces by Felicity Sidnell Reid
Towards the Pebbled Shore by Peter Jailall
Travels with Athóma by Daniel G Scott
Timed Radiance by Donna Langevin
Love and Lunch by Mori McCrae
Looking into the Fish Tank by Kent Bowman
The Frailty of Living Things by Carole Giangrande
Becoming History: A Life Told Through Poetry by Blaine Marchand
Bricolage: A Gathering of Centos by A. Garnett Weiss
The Mezzo Soprano Dines Alone by Thomas Gannon Hamilton
Earth's Signature: New & Selected Jackpine Sonnets by James Deahl
There is a Place by Ivy Reiss
Making Small Things Perfect by W.J. Keith
Dog Poems by Louise Carson
Clavier, Paris, Alyssum by Sue Chenette